Let's Make
Nice Cream

by Mari Bolte

NORWOOD HOUSE PRESS

Norwood House Press

For information regarding Norwood House Press, please visit our website at:
www.norwoodhousepress.com or call 866-565-2900.

PHOTO CREDITS: page 4: ©ellinnur bakarudin / Shutterstock; page 7: ©Archive Photos / Getty Images; page 8: ©taist2 /
Shutterstock; page 10: ©JeniFoto / Shutterstock; page 13: ©grandbrothers / Shutterstock; page 14: ©Photology1971 / Shutterstock;
page 15: ©Rosa Herrara; page 19: ©Rosa Herrara; page 21: ©Rosa Herrara; page 22: ©Rosa Herrara; page 23: ©Rosa Herrara;
page 24: ©Rosa Herrara; page 27: ©Rosa Herrara; page 28: ©chalermphon_tiam / Shutterstock

Hardcover ISBN: 978-1-68450-776-4
Paperback ISBN: 978-1-68404-755-0

LIBRARY OF CONGRESS CATALOGING-IN-PUBLICATION DATA
Library of Congress Cataloging-in-Publication Data has been filed and is available at catalog.loc.gov

353N—082022
Manufactured in the United States of America in North Mankato, Minnesota.

Contents

Ice cream and nice cream are both frozen, creamy treats that can be eaten in many ways.

All about Nice Cream

Is there anything better than cold ice cream on a hot day? It's delicious! Regular ice cream is made with **dairy** and sugar. But not everyone can have those things.

Nice cream is **vegan** ice cream. That means it doesn't have any animal products. It is also healthy! Nice cream is usually made with frozen bananas.

You don't need an ice cream maker, either. A blender or food processor makes nice cream in no time at all. Toppings, mix-ins, and flavor combinations mean there are endless types of nice cream to make.

People have been making frozen treats as far back as the second century BCE. That's more than 2,200 years ago. Ancient people flavored snow with honey, fruit, and syrup. The ice cream we enjoy today was first made in the 16th century, or around 500 years ago. Milk and cream were added to the mix. But only the rich and famous could afford to have it. It was another hundred years before other people got a taste.

By the early 1800s, people had invented ice houses. These **insulated** buildings kept things cold. Ice could be harvested from

This ice house was built in 1830 in Kentucky. It was used to keep ice cold year-round.

frozen lakes and stored for later use. The ice cream machine was invented in 1843. Both these inventions made it easier for people to enjoy ice cream. But they still had to eat the frozen treat before it melted. When home freezers were invented in the 1940s, people could finally have ice cream whenever they wanted.

Blenders and food processors are easy to use and easy to clean. Just be careful around the blades!

Blenders have been popular appliances in home kitchens since the 1950s. Food processors were invented in the early 1970s. Both are containers with spinning blades designed to **puree** food.

Immersion blenders look like handheld sticks. There is a handle on one end and a blender blade on the other. People can blend food in the bowl it is already in. Blenders and food processors are used to make smoothies, soups, sauces, and other blended dishes.

The invention of home appliances let people make their own ice cream at home. Tools such as blenders and food processors allowed people to get creative. Fruits could be pureed or chopped into fine bits. This gave people a new idea. What if they blended frozen bananas? Nice cream was created!

Bananas are one of the most popular fruits in America. They grew in popularity in the late 1800s. Bananas are inexpensive, low in calories, and full of nutrition. They are high in **fiber**, which helps you stay full for longer. And because they come in their own wrapper, they're easy to have on hand.

CHAPTER 2

Make Your Own Nice Cream

Fruit is full of water. When that water freezes, it turns into ice crystals. If fruit is frozen fast, the ice crystals that form are small. Small crystals mean the fruit will taste more like it does when it's fresh. The fruit is smoother when blended.

Large crystals lead to chunky, coarser blended fruit. It becomes mushy or watery as it melts.

Bananas have some of the lowest water content of all the fruits. When bananas freeze, their ice crystals are small. When frozen bananas are blended, those ice crystals are broken up to make smooth nice cream. Freezing the banana is important. Blending a room-temperature banana turns it into a thick liquid, not creamy nice cream.

Bananas have natural sugar and **pectin**. Pectin is what turns mashed fruit and sugar into wobbly, spreadable jam. It is also what keeps ice crystals small in order to make smooth nice cream. When bananas are blended, the pectin activates. It stops ice crystals from forming. It also makes nice cream airy and light.

Choosing the right banana is important. Green bananas are full of starch and **chlorophyll**. They are firm and feel waxy. Their flavor is

It takes about a week for a yellow banana to turn brown. Placing it inside a brown paper bag speeds up the process.

bitter too. It takes your body longer to **digest** an unripe banana. As the banana matures, the starches are turned into **simple sugars**. The banana gets softer, and the flavor gets sweeter. The chlorophyll is broken up, causing the banana peel to turn yellow, and then brown.

The more air that's blended into nice cream, the lighter and fluffier it will become.

Nice cream is a mixture of solid, liquid, and gas. The solid is the ice crystals. The liquid is whatever liquid you choose to blend with the banana. The gas is the air that is added when the bananas are blended. Using a blender or food processor is important when making nice cream. The spinning blades break the banana down and whip in air.

A little liquid is needed to help blend frozen fruit. You can use water, but that means more ice crystals will form. This will make your nice cream grainy. Dairy products or milk substitutes are mostly water, but they also have fats. Fats make nice cream creamier. They also help air bubbles form and keep the nice cream colder for longer.

Some milks have more fat than others. Heavy cream has the most fat. It will also give you a more ice cream-like texture. Coconut and cashew milk are good dairy-free alternatives.

You won't need much liquid to make nice cream. Start out with whatever you already have at home. You can always try something else later!

There are a few other things you will need. A container with an airtight lid is the most important. The air in the freezer pulls moisture out of frozen food. This makes ice crystals. The food dries out and is not pleasant to eat. This is called freezer burn.

You can flavor your nice cream. Extracts like almond or vanilla are nice. Syrups come in many flavors. Cocoa powder or flavored **protein** powder can also be stirred in. Spices like cinnamon and ginger are also delicious additions.

Mix-ins and toppings can add both flavor and texture. They can be stirred in or sprinkled on top. Chopped fruit or whole berries are healthy ideas. Nuts, sprinkles, coconut flakes, or crushed cookies can also be used. And don't forget whipped cream and a cherry on top!

Parts of Nice Cream

Nice Cream

Candy

Fruit

One small banana equals about 1/2 cup. Slice it into coins and place on a cookie sheet. This helps them freeze faster, making smaller ice crystals. Set the sheet in the freezer. Room-temperature bananas will just blend into liquid.

When your bananas are frozen, you can start blending. Have all of your ingredients ready. Also, have an adult help with chopping or crushing toppings and mix-ins.

Use a spoon to dish up your nice cream into a bowl. But to make the classic round scoop shape, you will need—surprise!—an ice cream scoop. Let your frozen nice cream sit out for a minute or two. Then, use a room-temperature scoop across the top. The scoop will warm the nice cream it touches just enough to create a smooth ball.

Materials Checklist

- ✓ 3–4 small bananas
- ✓ butter or dinner knife
- ✓ cookie sheet
- ✓ large bowl
- ✓ measuring cup
- ✓ blender, food processor, or immersion blender
- ✓ liquid, such as cream, milk, or milk substitute
- ✓ long spoon
- ✓ mix-ins, such as nuts, vanilla extract, or crushed candy
- ✓ ice cream scoop (optional)
- ✓ cone, dish, or jar
- ✓ toppings, such as fruit, whipped cream, or sprinkles
- ✓ airtight container

19

Safety in the kitchen is important. Always ask an adult for help with knives and other sharp tools.

CHAPTER 3

In the Kitchen!

Now that you know what goes into nice cream, it's time to make your own!

1. With an adult's help, prepare the bananas by cutting them into coins with a butter or dinner knife. Place the coins on a cookie sheet and freeze for 2 hours. You will also want to place the bowl in the freezer (to be used later).

2. Measure out 2 cups of frozen banana coins. Place them in a food processor or blending appliance of your choice.

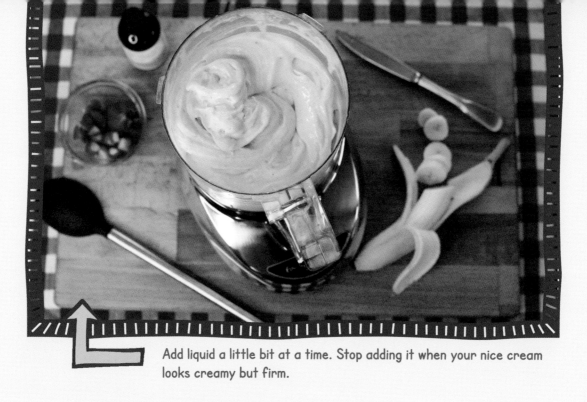

Add liquid a little bit at a time. Stop adding it when your nice cream looks creamy but firm.

3. Add the liquid 1 tablespoon at a time. Also add any mix-ins that will need to be well-blended, like a powder.

4. With an adult's help, blend the banana mixture until it is smooth. Add more liquid if the nice cream still looks chunky.

5. Use the long spoon to scoop the nice cream into the chilled bowl. Gently stir in any other mix-ins. Be quick—the longer your nice cream stays at room temperature, the faster it will melt.

6. You can eat your nice cream now if you prefer it more like soft serve. If you want it solid and scoopable like ice cream, freeze it for at least 30 minutes. Scoop frozen nice cream into a cone, dish, or jar.

7. If your nice cream is too hard to scoop, leave it out for a few minutes to soften.

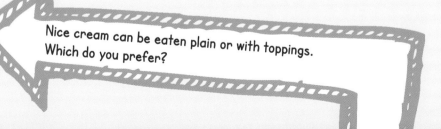

Nice cream can be eaten plain or with toppings. Which do you prefer?

8. Decorate your nice cream with toppings. Sprinkle on a few or add all your favorites!

9. Scoop any extra nice cream into the airtight container with an adult's help and store it in the freezer to enjoy later!

Enjoy your treat, and keep trying new ways to create this unique dessert. Your nice cream is limited only by your imagination!

Even Nicer!

Congratulations! You have made nice cream. Now see if there are ways to make it even better. Use any of these changes and see how they improve your nice cream.

- Don't like bananas? You can make nice cream with chickpeas instead! Chickpeas aren't as sweet as bananas. You'll have to add a natural sweetener, like maple syrup or agave. Chickpeas help the nice cream stay solid longer.

- Think about different ways you can eat nice cream. Nice cream pops, nice cream sandwiches, nice cream shakes, and nice cream cake are only a few ideas!

Can you think of any ways you could improve or change your nice cream to make it more to your liking?

Glossary

chlorophyll (KLOR-uh-fill): a green coloring found in all green plants

dairy (DARE-ee): something that contains, or is made from, milk

digest (DYE-jehst): to break down food in the body

fiber (FY-buhr): the parts of a plant your body can't digest or absorb

immersion (ih-MUR-zhuh): the act of plunging something, or being plunged, into liquid

insulated (IN-suh-lay-ted): covered up so heat cannot escape

pectin (PEK-tin): a thickening substance found in ripe fruits; pectin helps jams and jellies set

protein (PROH-teen): a part of certain foods, such as wheat, meat, and dairy products, that is important for healthy growth

puree (PYUR-ay): to blend something until smooth

simple sugars (SIM-puhl SHOO-guhrz): natural sweeteners found in fruits and milk

vegan (VEE-guhn): containing no animal products, such as meat or dairy

For More Information

Books

Bronski, Kelli. *Kids Cook Gluten-Free: Over 65 Fun and Easy Recipes for Young Gluten-Free Chefs*. New York, NY: The Experiment, 2022.

Elliot, Victoria Grace. *Yummy: A History of Desserts*. New York, NY: RH Graphic, 2021.

Tosi, Christina. *Milk Bar: Kids Only*. New York, NY: Clarkson Potter, 2020.

Websites

American Chemical Society (https://www.acs.org/content/acs/en/education/whatischemistry/adventures-in-chemistry/secret-science-stuff/ice-cream.html) An explanation of the science behind ice cream with facts and videos.

Kitchn: Wait, What is Nice Cream? (https://www.thekitchn.com/nice-cream-259557) History and recipes for nice cream.

National Geographic (https://youtu.be/SpAHPXNhAwk) A video history of bananas.

Index

About the Author

Mari Bolte has worked in publishing as a writer and editor for more than 15 years. She has written dozens of books about things like science and craft projects, historical figures and events, and pop culture. She lives in Minnesota.